To Stephen & Andrew.

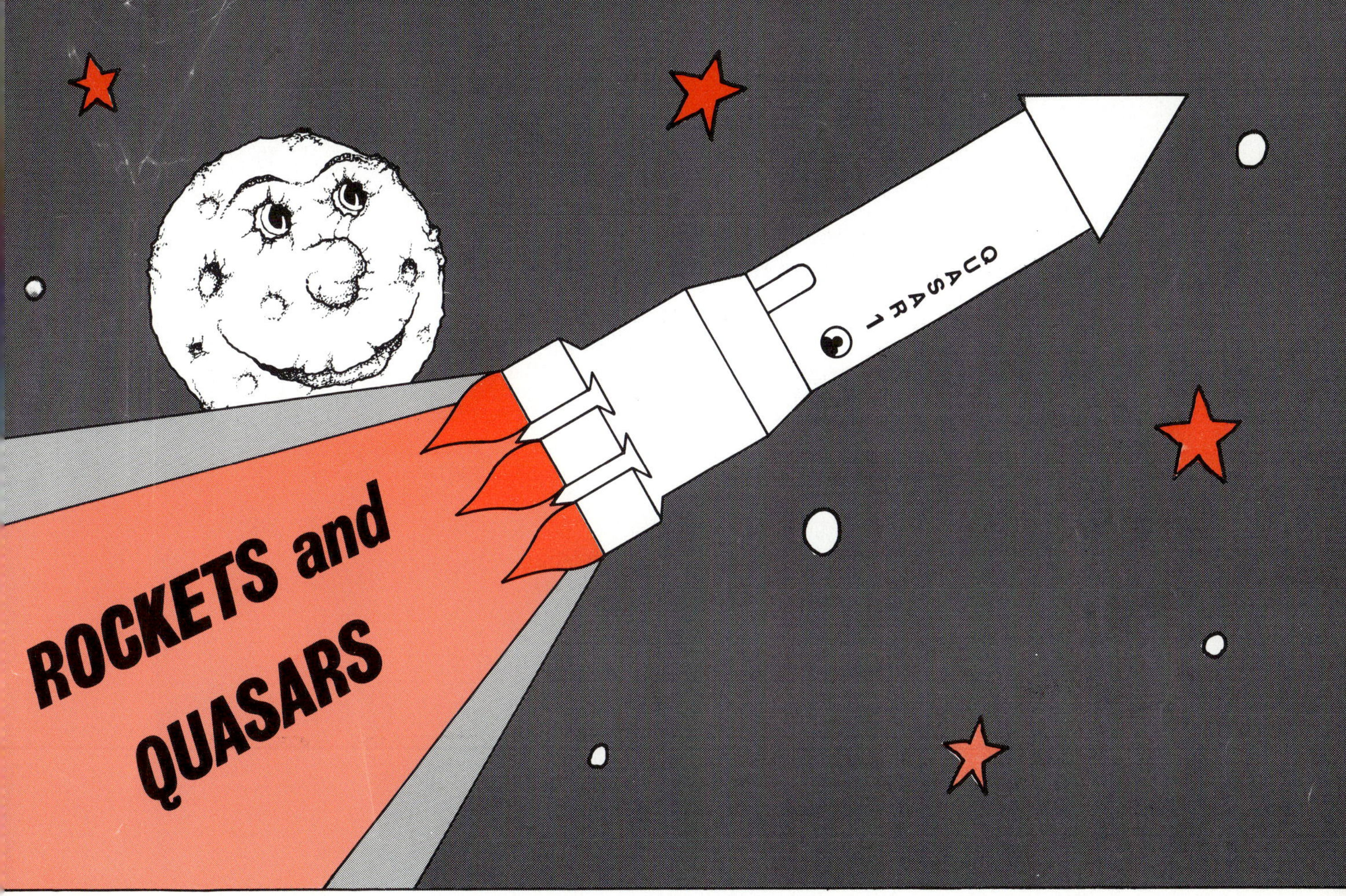

Poems for Children by **John Rice**

Illustrated by John Kneller

The Aten Press
47 Hendley Drive
Cranbrook
Kent

Other little children
Shall bring my boats ashore.

from 'Where Go the Boats?'
by Robert Louis Stevenson

For the Sunburst Kids, Jonathan, Stevie and René

British Library Cataloguing in Publication Data
Rice, John

Rockets and Quasars.
I. Title
821'.914 PZ8.3

ISBN 0 903633 08 6 (hardback)
ISBN 0 903633 09 4 (paperback)

First published in Great Britain 1984
by **The Aten Press, 47 Hendley Drive, Cranbrook, Kent.**

Printed by Flo-Print, Langton Green, Tunbridge Wells, Kent.

Contents:

For their active encouragement I'd like to thank Judy Miles BBC television producer who included some of these works in her 'English Resource Units' programmes; and to John Foster, Editor of the Oxford University Press poetry anthologies, where some of these poems appeared. Grateful thanks also go to Michelle Fink, Education Officer at the Poetry Society; Shelley, Owen and John at Flo-Print; and to Douglas Hall for his words of advice.

Brokendown
Countdown
Tense
Nice
Ates
Sonce
Sykes
Fice
Force
Thrice
Twice
Once
Nonce!!

If...

If ships sailed on the motorway
  And potato crisps were blue,
If football boots were made of silk
  And a lamp-post wore a shoe;
If motorbikes ran upwards
  And milk floats really floated,
If beds were full of boulders
  And peas were sugar-coated;
If flies wore bomber jackets
  And eggs laid little chickens,
If spacemen had a panther each
  And insects studied Dickens;
If babies' prams were motorised
  And you listened to your conscience,
If your brain was working properly
  You wouldn't read this nonscience!

Leisure Centre, Pleasure Centre

(for Aylesford Primary School)

Through plate glass doors
With giant red handles,
Into light that's as bright
As a million candles,
Chlorine smells, the whole place steaming
Kids are yelling, kids are screaming

Watch them wave jump
dive thump
cartwheel
free wheel
look cute
slip chute
toe stub
nose rub
in the leisure centre,
pleasure centre.

Sporty people laugh and giggle
Girls in swimsuits give a wiggle,
Kids in the cafe busy thinking
If they can afford some fizzy drinking,
In the changing rooms wet folk shiver
Hard to get dressed as you shake and quiver

And we go breast stroke
back stroke
two-stroke
big folk
hair soak
little folk
eye poke
no joke
in the leisure centre, pleasure centre.

And now we're driving back home
Fish and chips in the car,
Eyes are slowly closing
But it's not very far,
Snuggle wuggle up in fresh clean sheets
A leisure centre trip is the best of treats!

Because you can keep fit
leap sit
eat crisps
do twists
belly flop
pit stop
fill up
with 7-Up
get going
blood flowing
look snappy
be happy
in the leisure centre,
pleasure centre.

Dog Talk

Pebbles and shells
Water down wells
Churches and bells
Your dog smells.

Sand and waves
Bats in caves
Rants and raves
My dog behaves.

Beetles and slugs
Fleas in rugs
Kisses and hugs
Your dog's got bugs.

Keys and locks
Feet in socks
Eagles and hawks
My dog talks!

A chemistry student from Gillingham
Kept emptying jamjars and filling 'em
With a poisonous jelly
That was bright green and smelly
So he used it on teachers for killing 'em.

A Mouse in the Kitchen

There's a mouse in the kitchen
  Playing skittles with the peas,
He's drinking mugs of coffee
  And eating last week's cheese.

There's a mouse in the kitchen
  We could catch him in a hat,
Otherwise he'll toast the teacakes
  And that's bound to annoy the cat.

There's a mouse in the kitchen
  Ignoring all our wishes,
He's eaten tomorrow's dinner
  But at least he's washed the dishes.

Note
Yes, I'm the mouse in the kitchen
  Thank you for the grub,
I feel quite full but thirsty now
  So I'm nipping down the pub.

Shena Shovel

Shena Shovel the sheep shearer shouts
"My sheeps' eyes look so sunken,
I shut them sheep in the washing machine
But they come out short and shrunken!"

Shena Shovel the sheep shearer
Shampooed her sheep with shandy,
She shook and shrugged and shook them
Until their legs were bandy.

Shena Shovel the sheep shearer
Sharpened her shears with shocks
She surely shaved the sheepyshums
But she left them woolly socks.

In the Shed

"Get the spades and buckets from the shed."
said my father when we were getting ready
to go to the beach last Sunday.

I opened the shed door and
out fell my brother's cricket bat
out fell a pile of plastic plant pots
out fell the red lawn mower
out fell the red lawn mower's white cable
out fell my bike with the saddle missing
out fell an old doll wearing one shoe,
    blue pants and a woolly jumper
out fell a pair of rusty shears
out fell a cardboard box full of tennis balls
out fell Gogo the cat (he was sleeping
    in the cardboard box)
out fell two folded garden chairs
out fell another doll wearing trousers and a vest
out fell a smelly old blanket
out fell a smell old raincoat
out fell a smelly old person (we had
    wondered what had happened to Gran)
out fell a tea chest full of old rubbish
    including a lamp shade
    an old frisbee
    two scratched singles with no covers
    assorted shoes with no laces
    a brick
    a burst 1982 World Cup football
    some dolls house furniture
    lots of tatty old paperbacks
    (one with a dead bee stuck to the cover)
    a dirty towel
    more plastic plant pots
    and another old doll with no hair,
    one eye missing and a dummy in its mouth
out fell some old carpet with bugs in it
out fell the garden fork
out fell an old bike wheel
out fell a plastic bag full of wooden building bricks
out fell a load of paint tins (inside the paint had
    thick oozy skin on it)
out fell a doll that looked as if it had been
    drinking out of the paint tins
out fell a baking tray
out fell a pair of jeans
out fell a go-kart
and finally out fell three red buckets
    and three big spades with last year's sand
    still sticking to them.

Must clean that shed out sometime.

White socks, sports shoes

I'm a zippy little mover,

Track suit, headband

I'm like a supersonic hoover!

Hymn Number 43
God's Little Screechers

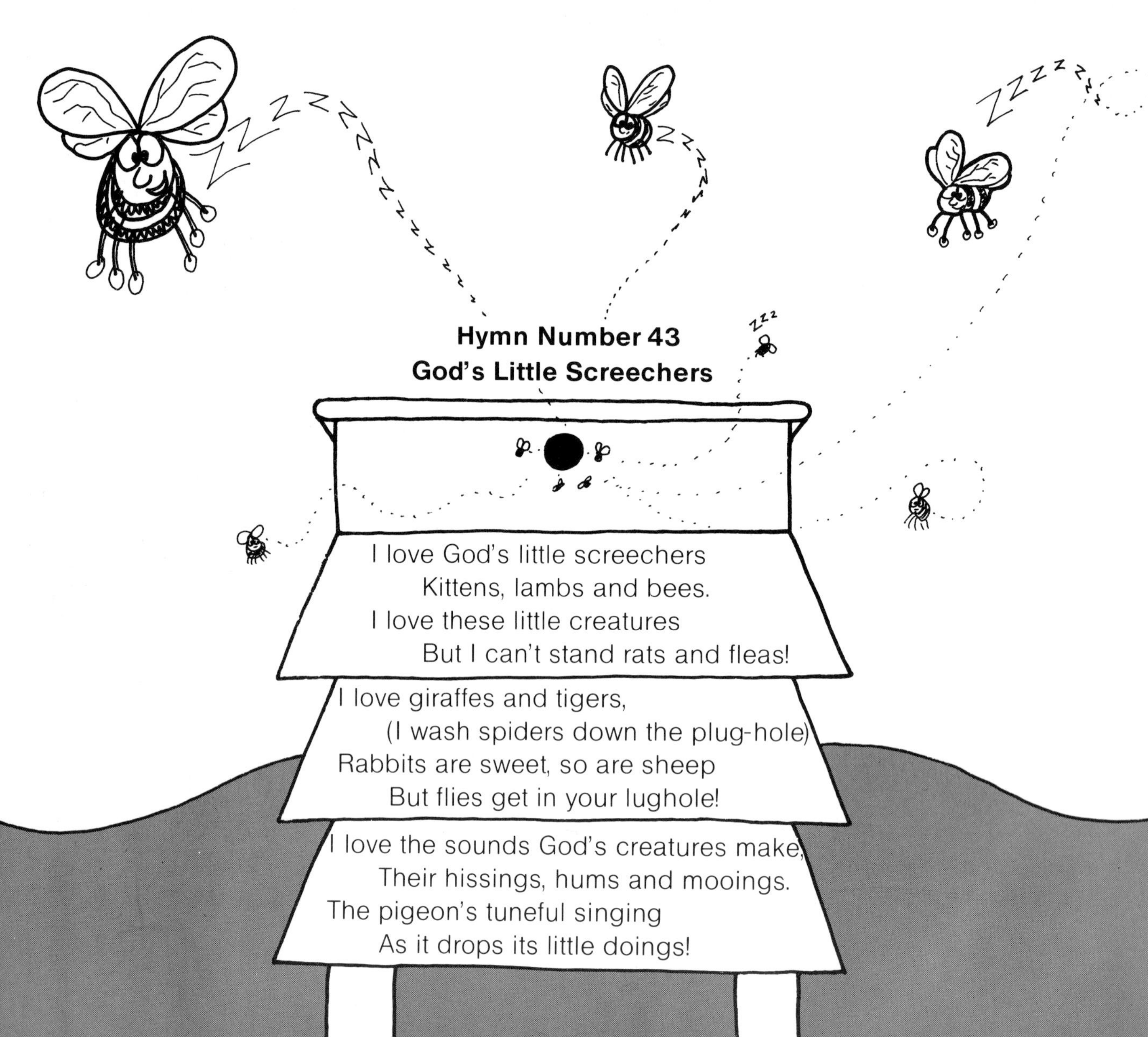

I love God's little screechers
Kittens, lambs and bees.
I love these little creatures
But I can't stand rats and fleas!

I love giraffes and tigers,
(I wash spiders down the plug-hole)
Rabbits are sweet, so are sheep
But flies get in your lughole!

I love the sounds God's creatures make,
Their hissings, hums and mooings.
The pigeon's tuneful singing
As it drops its little doings!

Two animals

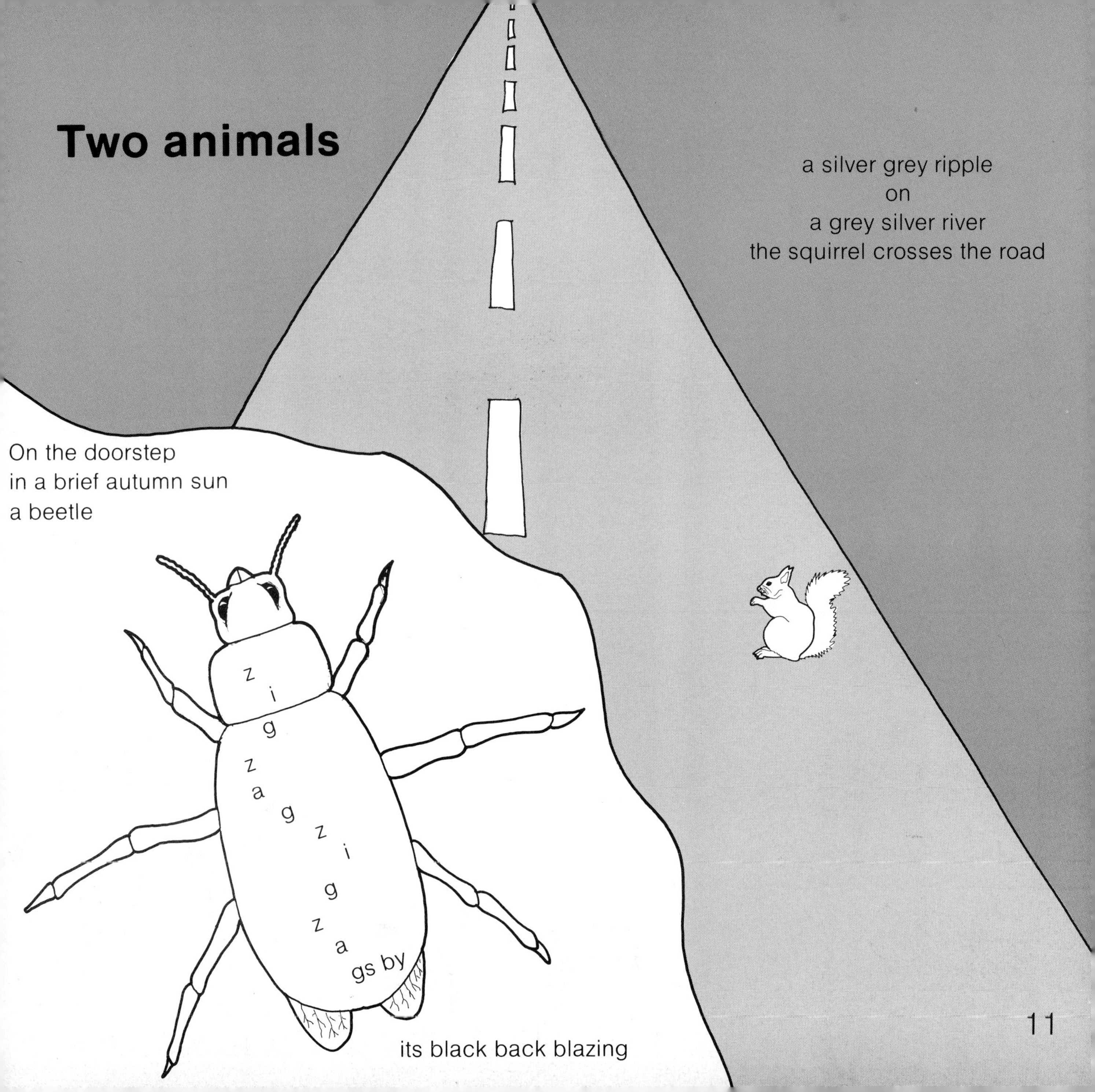

a silver grey ripple
on
a grey silver river
the squirrel crosses the road

On the doorstep
in a brief autumn sun
a beetle
zigzagzigzags by

its black back blazing

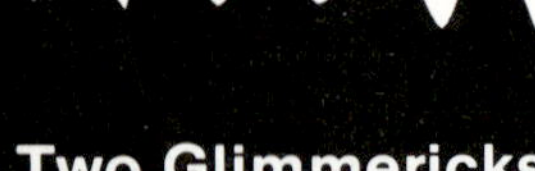

Two Glimmericks

Susanna Kavanagh scoffed a sultana
Then burped on a fat banana
  She would guzzle more soon,
  If she could find a large spoon
Instead of using a spanner.

* * *

On a country walk in a very thick mist
My girlfriend asked if I'd give her a kiss,
  But I missed her lips
  Because of the fog
And I kissed her little one-eyed dog.

Tongue Tied Teeth

Does a duck lack socks?
Can a crab drag flags?
Can a doll kiss moss,
Or a rabbit rip rags?

Will a quick queen quack
While a chick chops chips?
Can a fish dash back
Before the gruff stag trips?

Do three thin thrushes
Slap plums in a beech?
Can ten red tramps
Fetch such a rich peach?

Can a sweet sheep's feet
Creep through green grass?
Can six pigs' legs
Shine sharp as brass?

Did the king swing string?
Has the moon cool boots?
Does a sink drink ink?
Have spruce trees roots?

I've a wooden cooken booken
That can sing a soft song,
I'd ding you up for dinner
But my gong's donged wrong!

(Most of the words in this poem came from Janet and John books)

Join me in an edinburga

A seagull who never liked soaring
Thought gliding was also quite boring
So he perched on his ledge
And built a big sledge
Which he used when the weather was snowring!

Everyone knows that kind of poem is called a 'limerick' (or glimmericks as I call them). I am proud to tell you that I have invented a new kind of short poem which is like a limerick only it is much dafter!
My new kind of verse is called an 'edinburga'. Here's an example:

Two schoolgirls who were searching for conkers
Found a tiger reading a comic
They asked for its autograph
On a shiny photograph
But he only frowned and said "Don't be stupid,
tigers can't write, are you bonkers?"

Now I know it doesn't scan, or flow or rhyme very well – but that's the point edinburgas aren't supposed to! A good edinburga should dress up like a limerick but must never be one. Oh yes, and one more thing: it is very important that an edinburga should be as mad and as crazy as can be – otherwise it will just be a bad limerick in disguise.

Follow these rules to make your own edinburgas:

1) **edinburgas must not scan very well**
2) **edinburgas must not rhyme very well**
3) **edinburgas must be as mad as can be!**

As you can probably tell, edinburgas can be written by even the worst poets in the world! In fact the best (or should I say worst), well the best worst edinburgas are usually written by the worst poets in the world. All you need to write the perfect edinburga is to be a very bad poet who is absolutely nutty! You seem to fit that description so have a go.

Here's one more example of a really ~~awful~~ terrific edinburga:-

Some spacemen on Mars were playing football
When an alien being appeared on the pitch
"What do you want alien –
A kick up the spalien?" (That's Martian for 'bum')
No I just wondered if you'd scratch my itch.

Brilliant eh?

WHAT A LOAD OF GRUBBISH!!!

In Church

The old bellringer
goes ding-dang-dong.
The boys in the choir
sing a sing-sang-song.
The vicar tells the people
do no wring-wrang-wrong.
Church mice on cushions
go bing-bang-
booiinngg.

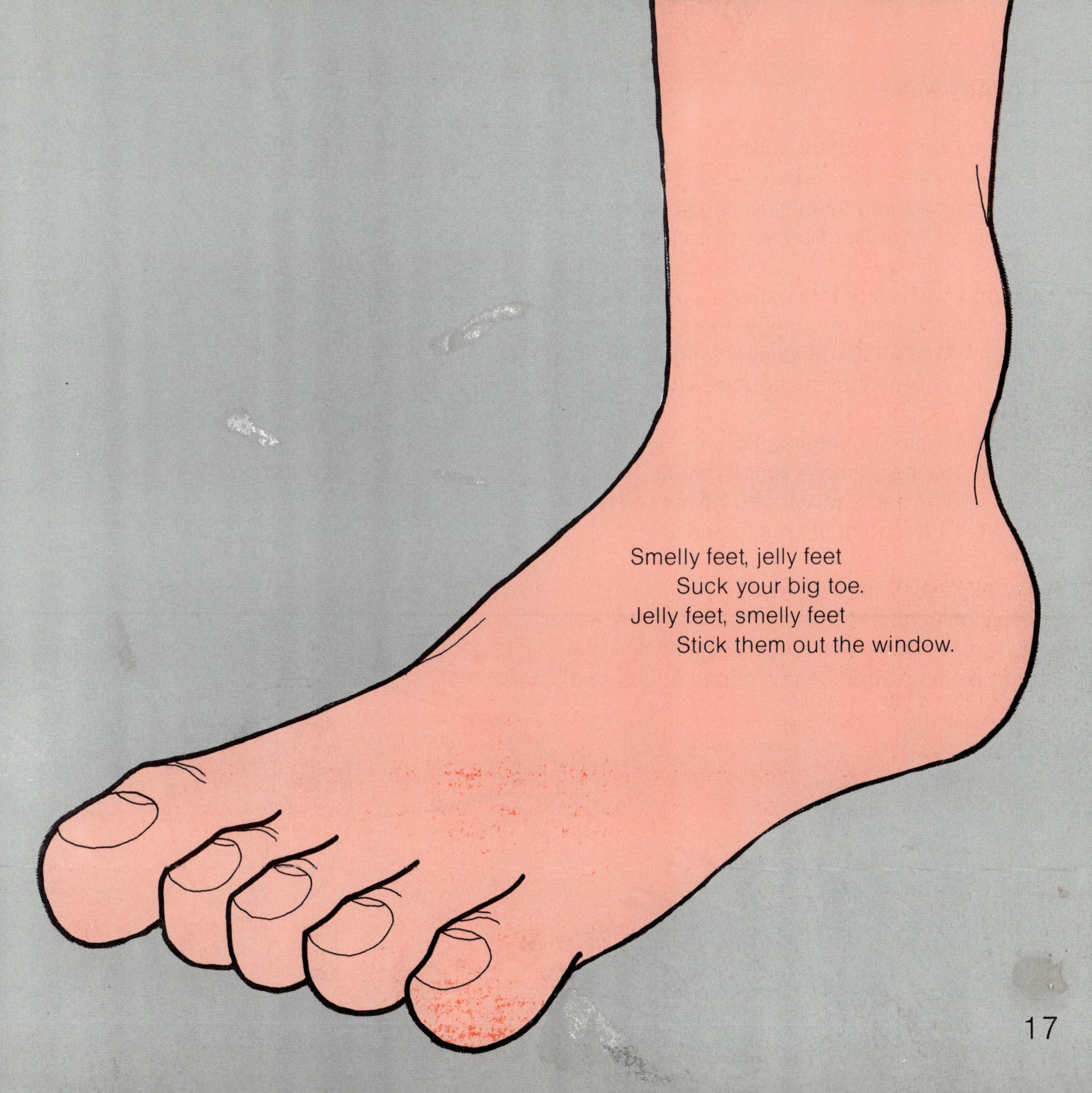

Smelly feet, jelly feet
Suck your big toe.
Jelly feet, smelly feet
Stick them out the window.

Country walks

Country walks, country walks
Every weekend it's country walks.
Over barbed wire fences ripping your socks
My parents are fanatical about country walks!

Country walks, country walks
I'm sick and tired of country walks,
I mean what about beaches – what about the docks
You never see ships on country walks!

Country walks, country walks
All we ever get is more country walks.
You seldom see a rabbit, you **never** see a fox
So what's the point of country walks?

Country walks, country walks
You won't catch me on any more country walks.
So rats to nature and farmers in smocks
Stuff them up your jumper, stupid country walks!

A Pen Beside Us

When I woke up from my anaesthetic
I must have looked really pathetic,
My movements were jerky, my thoughts were erratic
My head was spinning like a Hoovermatic.

When I came round from my operation
I felt as lonely as a railway station
I had gained a scar and lost an appendix
Thank goodness it's gone, it looked really horrendix.

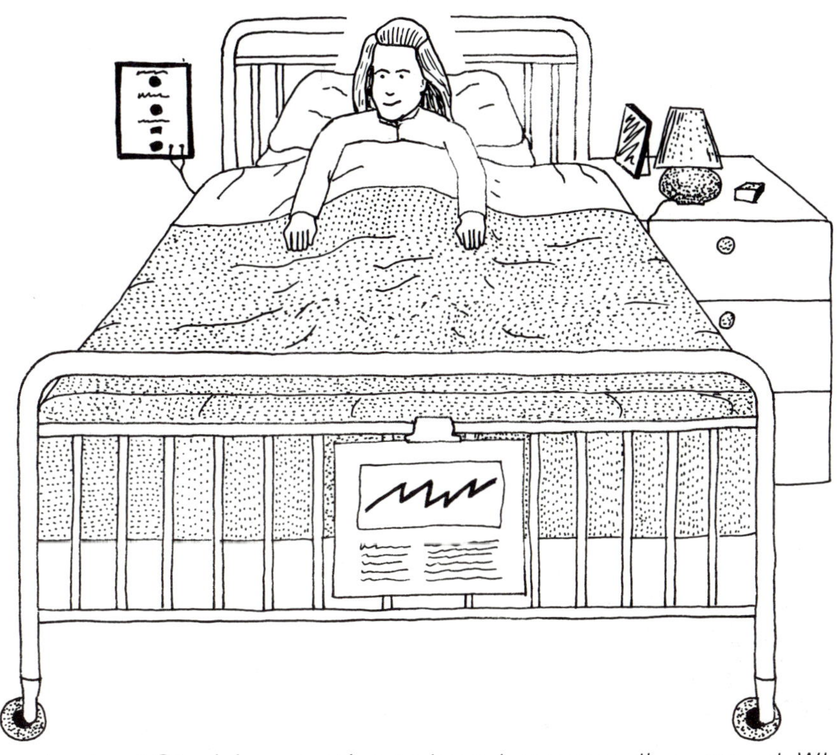

(This poem is about Stevie's operation to have her appendix removed. When I told people she had Appendicitis they thought I said 'A Pen Beside Us')

Next Door's Cat

Next door's cat has a stripey coat
He also wears black wellies,
He lost his thermal underwear
So now he borrows Nelly's.

Next door's cat has a bath each night
He dives into the basin,
We keep a saucer full of milk
For him to wash his face in.

When I was going to a party . . .

When I was going to a party
(As I have already said in the title)
I saw our cat Gogo
(Who is big and fat and orange and has only one eye)
Sitting on a parked car six streets away
From our house.

All through the party I was worried in case
He couldn't find his way home.
Several times I managed to get knocked out
Of games so that I could look out of the window
To see if he had followed me, but no.

The party finished at 9 o'clock
So I was home before the news finished.
Just as I was going off to bed
I noticed the cat's dish under the stairs:
The fish had been eaten.

I slept happily and dreamt I was a pop star.

Two Ghosts

She shakes me just before
dawn goes on duty.

"I dreamt that every day
when I wasn't there,
a little teddy walked under my bed.
When I came in it fell over
and stopped walking."

At first it all sounded logical
since I myself thought this was a dream:
but her small voice is full of worry
and I know why she's here.
The night is so big.

We go downstairs to talk
of god, ghosts and dead things.
She drinks Coca-Cola and I drink Lucozade
hoping to avoid being one of the
the dead things too soon.

After a time we return to bed.
In the brightening morning
we glide quietly upstairs –
we look like our own ghosts.

I skim her cheek with a kiss
saying: "Go back to sleep now."
I feel pleased that I have
brushed away her cares
with a father's reassurance.

"Yes," she answers, "but I'll just
have one look under the bed."

I am.... star counting

I am . . . lying here counting the stars
that sparkle through my bedroom window.
For years now I've watched them
On winter nights when my eyes grow tired of reading.

So I open the curtain, turn off the light
and tune into the dark.
The stars' light pierces the glass like ice-light
And I start counting.

One ... two ... three ... four ... plus three on Orion's belt ...

By the time my eyes close for sleep
I'm already at eleventyteen thousillion ...

It's too dark to write it down,
Not to worry, I'll start again tomorrow night.

Sun stuff

Sun stuff, star fluff
There is laughter in space.

Moon light, laser bright
Rockets zoom anyplace.

Meteor sigh, comet cry
Space night dark and cold.

Planet breeze, solar freeze
Our universe grows old.

A Really Unextraordinary Misadventure

(After V.M.)

I screamed at the moon
"Come up ...
Come up you fatsobatso sometimes skinnymalinky
White orange!"
I screamed at the moon.

"All day you sleep behind China
While I have to work here
Scribbling notes, writing things upon things upon things."
I screamed at the moon
"Now just you look here dusty-eyes,
Instead of appearing every night
Why not come out one morning
And have corn flakes with me!"

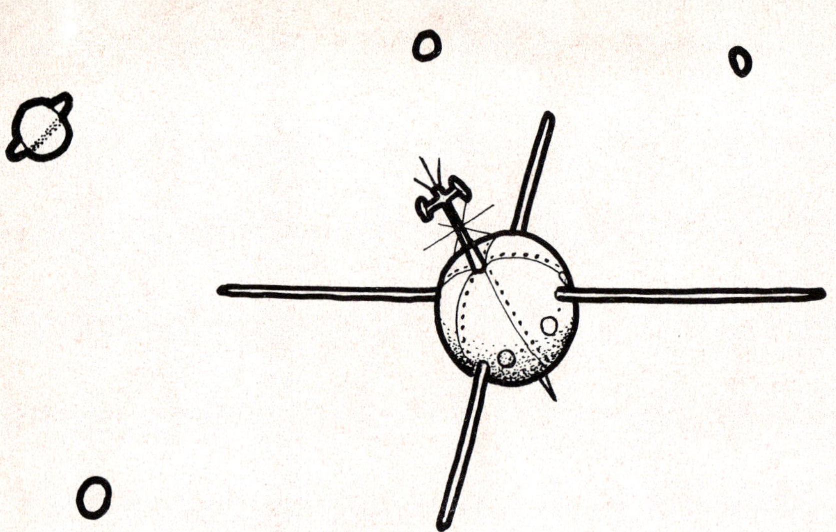

Rhyme of the Modern Mariner

"From Venus to Pasadena
I send you all you wish to know"

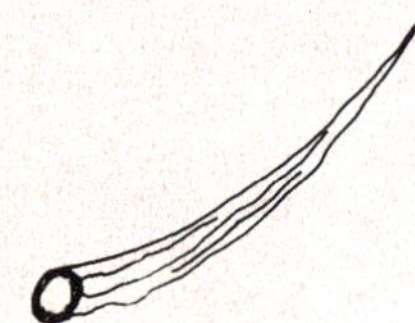

Temperatures, pressures, atmospheric conditions –
but no account of the view.
From my regular communications
you can calculate the length of a Venusian day,
or determine the density of its surface atmosphere.
But how can I express to you
the beauty and riddle of this planet's Ashen Light
when its dark bulk fits baby snug in the crescent cradle.

No, I cannot transmit such rich information
in computer code through cold spaceways
so I shall hold these sights in my Mariner mind
and travel endless through the solar system
carrying an unwritten song from
some dreamer's morning.

On Some Other Planet

On some other planet
near some other star,
there's a music-loving alien
who has a green estate car.

On some other planet
on some far distant world,
there's a bright sunny garden
where a cat lies curled.

On some other planet
a trillion miles away,
there are parks and beaches
where the young aliens play.

On some other planet
in another time zone,
there are intelligent beings
who feel very much alone.

On some other planet
one that we can't see,
there must be one person
who's a duplicate of me.

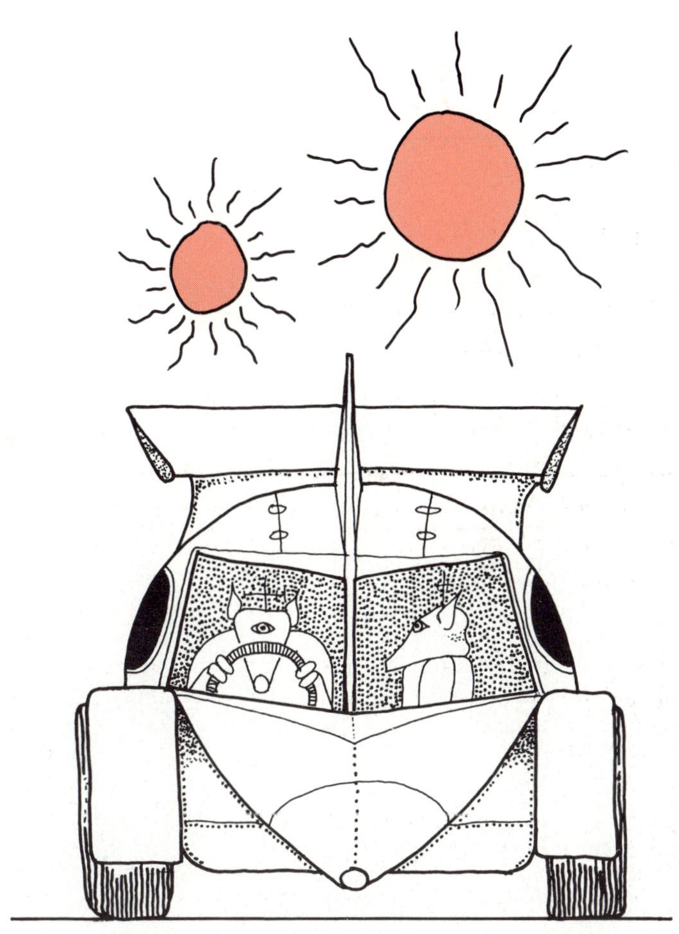

Time You Did

Dawn is the only time
Birds get for rehearsing new songs.

Day is when people and vehicles
Cruise like lost submarines.

Evening could deafen you
If everyone turned their TVs up full volume.

Night is the only time
Shy animals get to windowshop.

First day of spring

First day of spring,
a girl and two boys
are mending a puncture.

The weak sun spikes the water
in the basin
and the bubbles from
the submerged inner tube
rise up like tiny, transparent balls.

Spanners, oil can, repair kit,
spoons and screwdrivers all lie
on the pavement warming their winter metal.

A girl and two boys
are mending a puncture
under a thin cloud
beside nodding daffodils
a new bike for a new yellow year.

Dull Thursday

It's a dull Thursday.
The clouds are sloping around the sky
looking for trouble.
The house is as quiet as words shut in a book.

One is out playing tennis:
One is visiting Sian:
One is at the pictures:

It's a dull Thursday.
Looking for something to do
I bring in the washing – it's only half dry,
I hoover up the living room,
I tidy the bookshelves,
I play some old records.

I hate dull Thursdays.

They'll be home in about an hour:
Suppose I could plug in the Atari,
I could make some toast,
I could go back to bed even.
But there's no fun in any of these.

Wander upstairs, open the drawer
bring out photographs of us:
this one on the beach at Camber Sands,
this one with Tom and Val in Padstow,
some Christmas shots,
photos of our house, our cat, our family,
when there were blue skies, bright colours
and dull Thursdays were never even heard of.

I hate dull Thursdays –
worse than that I hate being alone.

Action Stations

Bend your elbows
When making the bed
The child fell over
And cracked her head.

They sent for the doctor
The undertaker too
And they buried her deep
Next to old Bill Drew.

(Make up some actions for this rhyme)

Noises Off

Ever been kissed by a toothless vampire?
    (gwaaalll-smacktup)
Ever thrown water on a Brownies' campfire?
    (splutsch-frisskress-kik)

Ever caught your socks on a rusty wire?
    (pir-keressfrick-twick)
Ever found and rolled an old tractor tyre?
    (coom-coom-roooo-rooo-roo-roo-roooodth)

Ever jumped in a barrel for a cooling drink?
    (whee-sklundftlslansh-blurburb-drok)
Ever bathed a baby in the kitchen sink?
    (splumge-splumge-thwogt-bunk-dribbledub)

Ever smashed a clock with a heavy hammer?
    (who-powcrunchaduncklecrash-tinkle-bink-ink-k)
Ever heard a referee with a stutter and stammer?
    (wh . . . wh . . . whis . . . whistle)

(Get a friend to make the noises while you recite the poem)

Dark Shark Lark

Frig frag frogman
Dives in the deep,
Flop flap flippers
Fixed to his feep.

Ship shape sharkle
Jaws open wide,
Snip snap snorkle
Frogman died.

(Recite this poem holding your nose)

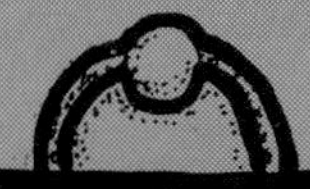

Daze of the Weak

All children to receive pocket money today:	M . . . . day
Shoes to be cleaned only once per week, today:	S . . . . day
Marriages may be conducted today (funerals too provided it's after 10 pm):	W . . . . day
Everyone must talk to a fir tree today:	F . . . day
Compulsory fish & chips for tea today:	F . . . day
Everyone must run rings round someone else today:	S . . . . . day
No work, no school so the weather must be good today:	S . . . . day

(Fill in the spaces and make up the Daze of the Weak)

Muntze of the Ear

Jan you are Ray in disguise.

Fair brewery does not always mean fair beer.

Marge is easier to spread than butter.

Ape reel is not a film about King Kong.

Mare is pronounced the same as 'mayor'.

Dune is where sand grains gang up on the sea.

Jewel eye doesn't mean see-through diamonds.

A gust of wind blew right through my ears.

Accept timber if you ordered bricks but only wood was available.

Och Tober is a Scottish way of saying 'Oh dash!'

No Farnborough airshow this year due to Jumbo on the runway.

Does amber mean stop on traffic lights?

(Read this out loud to a friend and you'll discover the Muntze of the Ear)

Two Twongue Twiztas

At midday on Mayday the maid May
made homemade marmalade.

* * *

Do you refutiter or disputiter
that a hootiter on a scootiter
can pollutiter the neutiter transmutiter
in your computiter?
No, well you must be stupiter than Jupiter!

Apples slap, bananas slope
Wash your face with sausage soap.

Peaches scream, pineapples scratch
Submarines sink so shut the hatch.

If your roly poly jelly
Falls splat on the floor,
Take your shoes and socks off
And kick it out the door!

I know a history teacher
Whose name is Miss McVicars,
She wears football boots and a gas mask
And great big baggy . . . jumpers.

(Can you think of a better final rhyme for this little verse?)

Play on Words

Here's a restaurant scene you can act with one of your friends:

Customer: (reading small menu) Have you got any lemons in their denims?

Waiter/ Waitress: Sorry, I don't think we have any lemons in their **denims.**

Customer: What about peaches in their parkas. Got any of them?

Waiter/ Waitress: Very sorry, we don't sell peaches in their parkas.

Customer: Now surely you can serve me gherkins in their jerkins.

Waiter/ Waitress: Sorry, no can do.

Customer: My hat! What kind of restaurant is this! Now surely you can fetch me some aubergines in overcoats?

Waiter/ Waitress: I don't even know what an aubergine looks like!

Customer: Well it's sort of purply with green bits... it looks like a stretched apple, but look, never mind all this – just bring me a dish of truffles in their duffles!

Waiter/ Waitress: I'm afraid I can't do that.

Customer: Don't tell me you don't sell truffles.

Waiter/ Waitress: On the contrary, we **do** sell truffles but I'm afraid we're out of duffles.

Customer: (getting really mad) Oh this is just ridiculous, for goodness sake just tell the cook to fix me a plate of banapples in their anoraks!

Waiter/ Waitress: I'm very sorry, I didn't catch what you said.

Customer: (shouts) BANAPPLES IN THEIR ANORAKS.

Waiter/ Waitress: I thought that's what you said. (pause) Banapples. Would that be (spells) B-A-N-A-P-P-L-E-S?

Customer: Stop showing off, so what if you're a good speller, go and get me something to eat.

Waiter/ Waitress: (slopes off mumbling) Banapples in their anoraks, huh. Peaches in parkas, gee whiz...

(returns to customer) Sorry, cook says it would take too long to crossbreed a banana with an apple and even if we could we wouldn't know whether to unzip it or peel it.

Customer: (furious) Well, what does your cook intend to feed me? You don't seem able to cater for my rather specialised taste!

Waiter/ Waitress: Well cook did ask me to bring you this more traditional dish with the restaurant's compliments.

Customer: Oh really and just what is this great delicacy? After all you don't have lemons in denims, nor peaches in parkas, nor gherkins in jerkins, not even aubergines in overcoats, nor truffles in duffles – you don't even have banapples in anoraks. So what have you got?

Waiter/ Waitress: Potatoes in their jackets.

Skipping Rhyme

Netball
Setball
I had a soaking wet doll

Netball
Letball
Her name was Rosie Letfall

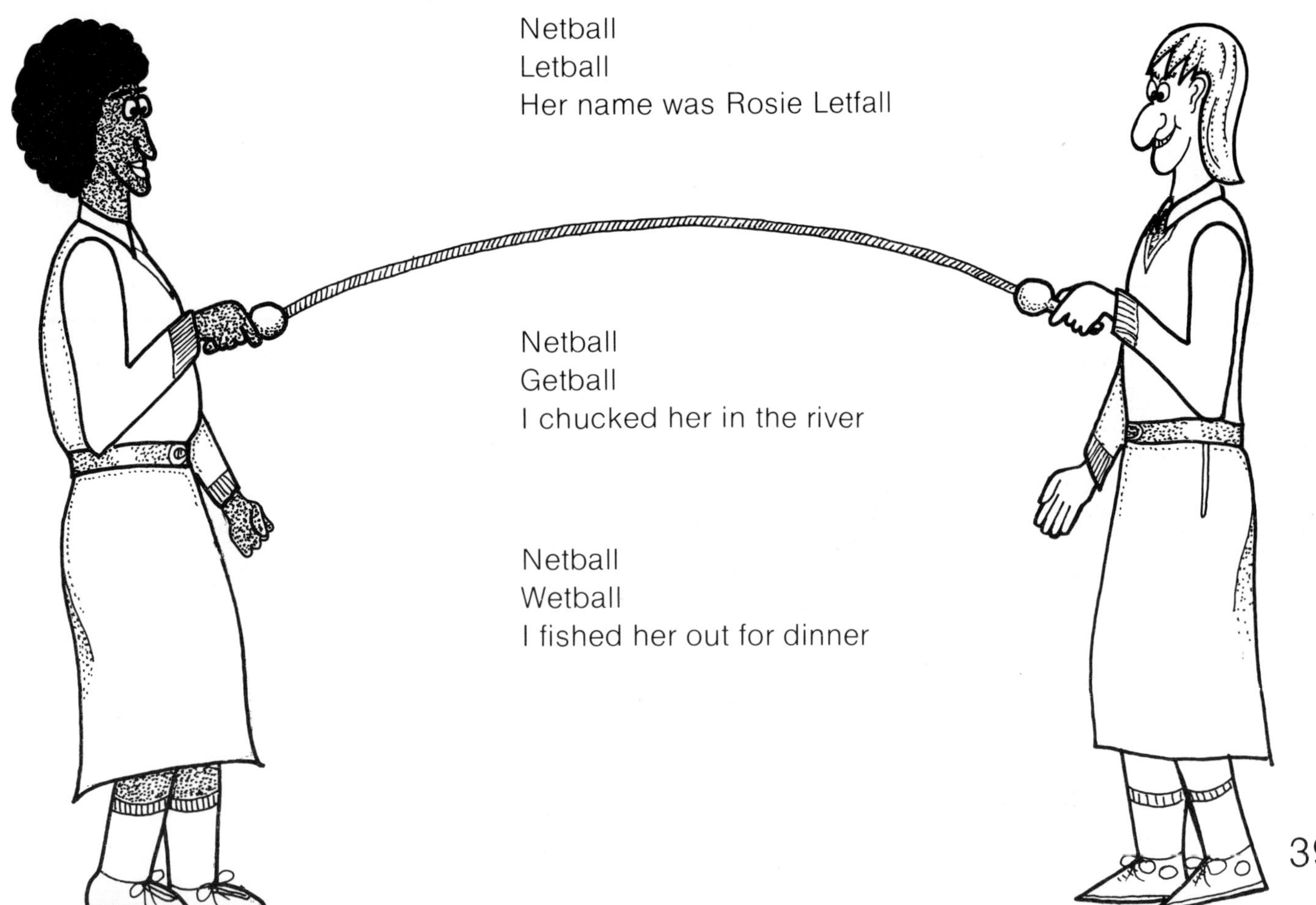

Netball
Getball
I chucked her in the river

Netball
Wetball
I fished her out for dinner

Pull your trolley, push your pram
The supermarket shelves are crammed with jam.

Peddle your bike, paddle your boat
I married a pig who got my goat.

Turn your key, start your car
Girls stay single if you want to go far.

Apple Jingle, Japple Angle

Pickem Packem
Stickem Stackem
Apples in a Box

Bitem Munchem
Lickem Crunchem
A Pippin and a Cox.

Top Ten

Ten little pop stars bopping in a line
One went on a world tour then there were nine.
Nine little pop stars rapping at the gate
One joined a reggae band then there were eight.
Eight little pop stars rocking under heaven
One appeared on Top of the Pops then there were seven.
Seven little pop stars released a disco mix
One broke his guitar strings then there were six.
Six little pop stars performing on stage live
One got into heavy metal then there were five.
Five little pop stars boogie on the floor
One got lost in a video film then there were four.
Four little pop stars sing "Baby stay with me"
One became a DJ then there were three.
Three little pop stars rocking at the zoo
A tiger ate the drumkit then there were two.
One little pop star a guitar in his hand
His record got to No. 1 but he's lost his favourite band.

Song of the Starving Dinner Ladies

Greenflies, gulls' beaks, gizzard of gnu
    Mix them well Mrs Stodge
We want a lovely sticky stew.

Rubber bands, bits of string sprinkled with confetti
    Stir it well Mrs Slop
We'll convince them it's spaghetti.

Blobs of yellow Dulux paint, fluff off a duster
    Simmer gently Mrs Sludge
We don't want lumpy custard.

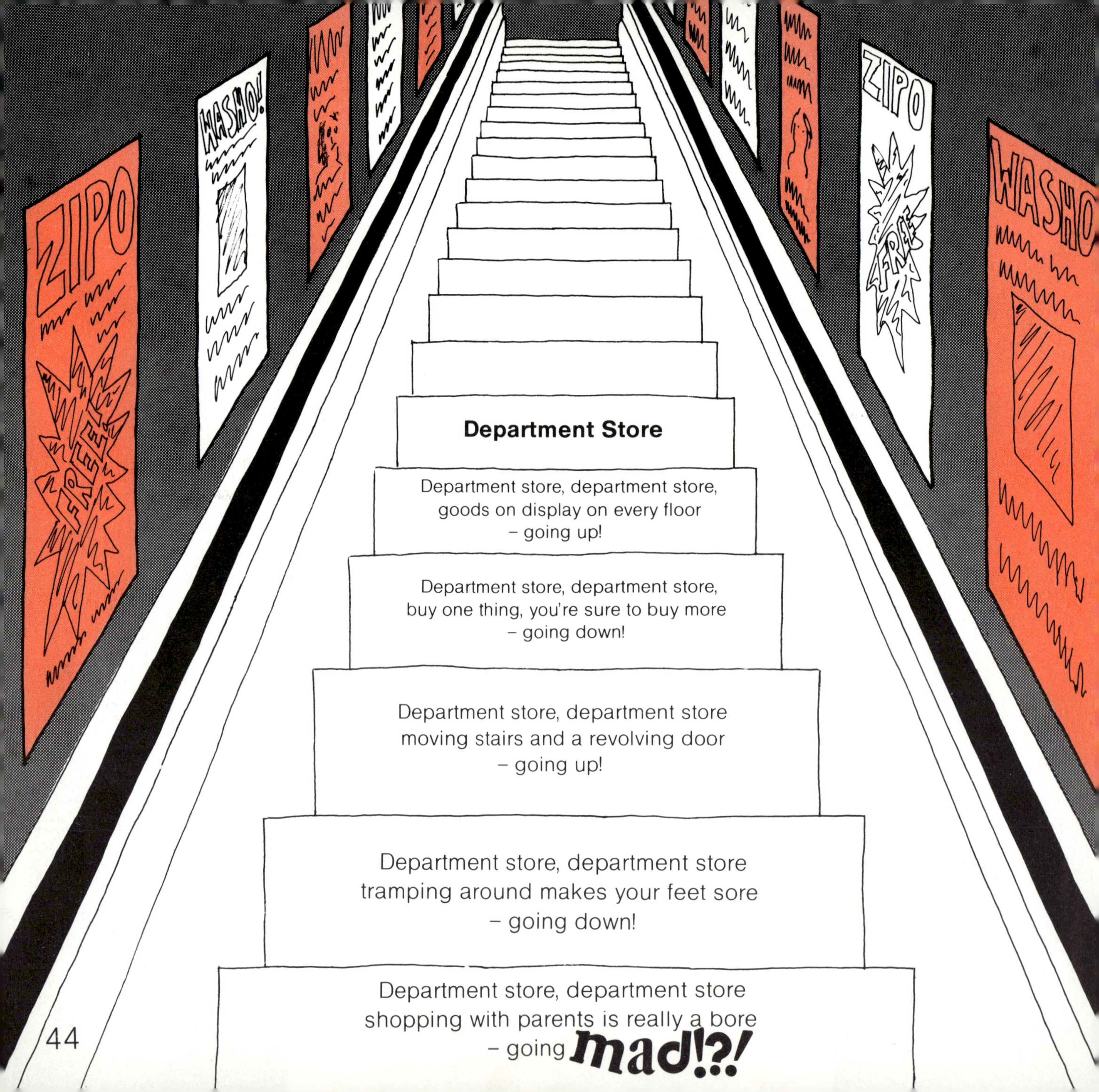

Department Store

Department store, department store,
goods on display on every floor
– going up!

Department store, department store,
buy one thing, you're sure to buy more
– going down!

Department store, department store
moving stairs and a revolving door
– going up!

Department store, department store
tramping around makes your feet sore
– going down!

Department store, department store
shopping with parents is really a bore
– going **mad!?!**

Now to tell what tomorrow's weather will be like, here's our new BBC forecast presenter, Claudia Wetha

Tomorrow there will be bright periods
over Northern Scotland followed by
scattered flowers over the Outer Hebrides.
Over much of the southern part of Britain
there will be dew and frost, mist and frog
sleet and snow, soot and smog.
Inland it will be cool but
outland it will be really uncool, man.
Eastern districts will start fine but
patchy cloud will develop with squally showers.
This will be followed by patchy trousers and
squelchy pillows.

Over much of Ireland
the sun won't be very bright
and the day will be dull.
There will be dense cloud and
the fog will be pretty thick too.

Over South Eastern regions
it will rain cats and dogs in buckets.
Thunder will clap and tidal waves will have
a whale of a time.
Tornadoes will ruin the tomatoes,
Volcanoes will pulverize Volkswagons,
An American hurricane will be asked
to hurrycane uppicane soonicane
and at sea most mast mist must clear immediately
if the lookout is to see where he's going.

Rain will lash down, winds will whip up
and thunder will crack. There will be
circus clouds all over the place.

That is the end of the whether forecast
because we don't know whether it will be
rainy or sunny, dull or fine, cloudy or clear.

I'm under so much pressure,
I'm in a state of depression.

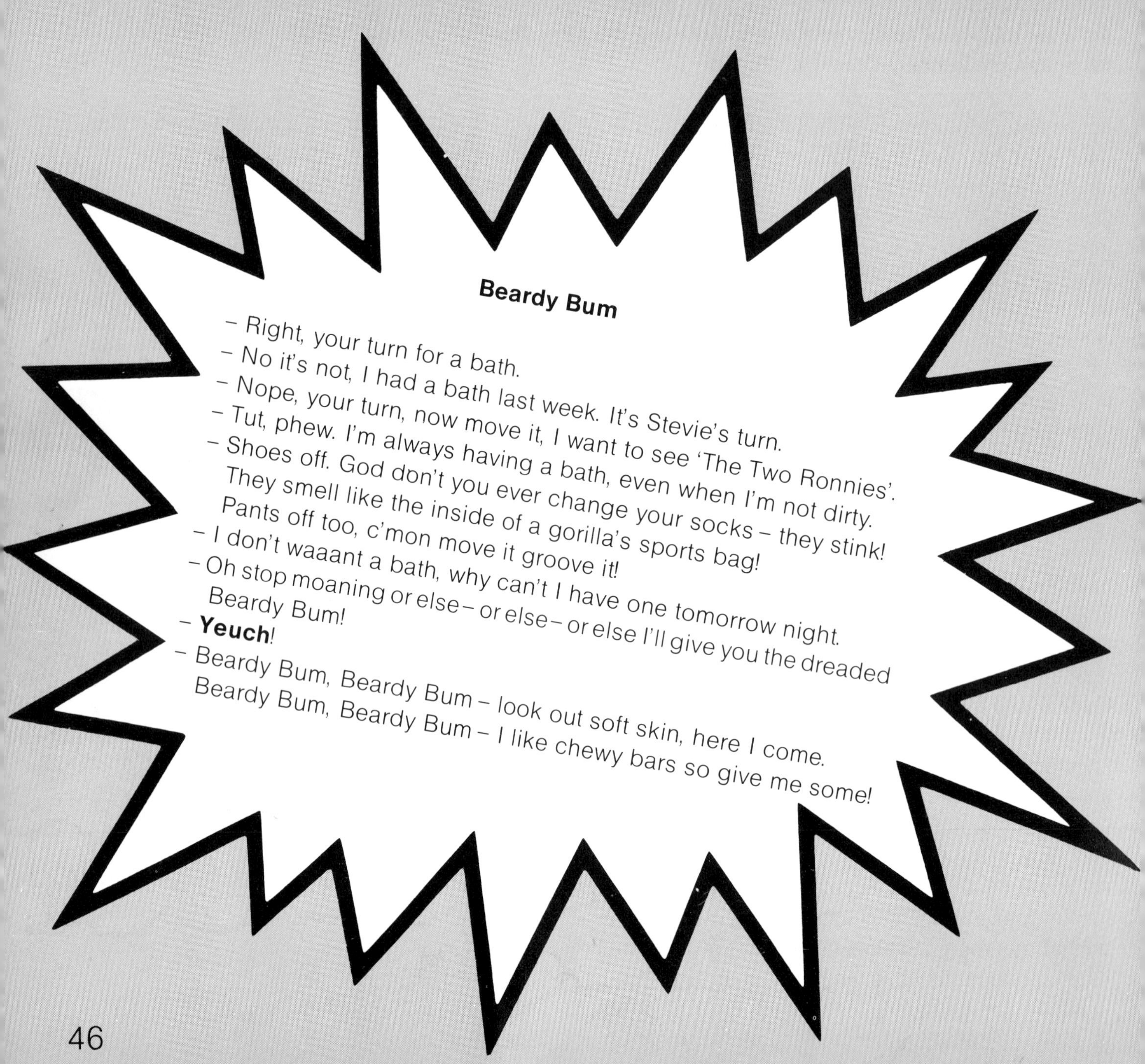
Beardy Bum
– Right, your turn for a bath.
– No it's not, I had a bath last week. It's Stevie's turn.
– Nope, your turn, now move it, I want to see 'The Two Ronnies'.
– Tut, phew. I'm always having a bath, even when I'm not dirty.
– Shoes off. God don't you ever change your socks – they stink!
They smell like the inside of a gorilla's sports bag!
Pants off too, c'mon move it groove it!
– I don't waaant a bath, why can't I have one tomorrow night.
– Oh stop moaning or else – or else – or else I'll give you the dreaded
Beardy Bum!
– **Yeuch**!
– Beardy Bum, Beardy Bum – look out soft skin, here I come.
Beardy Bum, Beardy Bum – I like chewy bars so give me some!

Paula Plughole

In a bathtub one Saturday evening
Paula Plughole was scrubbing her foot,
  As the water turned dirty
  She became very shirty
She'd forgotten to take off her boot!

For some time she fought to remove it
Then lay back for a well earned rest,
  But her patience was lost,
  And she became very cross
When she noticed she still wore her vest!

"Oh I wish I'd undressed to my skin."
Said Paula the most bedraggled of sights,
  "There'd be no need to thrash,
  To splunge or to splash
And I wouldn't have soaking wet tights!"

Big Fears

Twenty-five feet above Sian's house
hangs a thick wire cable
that droops and sags between two
electricity pylons.
A notice says it carries 40,000 volts
from one metallic scarecrow to the next,
then on to the next and the next
right across the countryside to the city.
The cable sways above Sian's council house
making her radio crackle and sometimes
making her television go on the blink.

If it's a very windy night
Sian gets frightened because she
thinks the cable might snap,
fall onto the roof and electrocute
everyone as they sleep.

This is Sian's Big Fear.

Outside Matthew's bedroom there
is a tall tree. Taller than the house.
In summer it is heavy with huge leaves.
In winter it stands lonely as a morning moon.
On a windy night, Matthew worries
that the tree might be blown down
and crash through his bedroom window.
It would certainly kill him and his cat
if it wasn't in its own cardboard box.

This is Matthew's Big Fear.

Outside Karen's bedroom there's nothing
but a pleasant view: meadows, hedges, sheep
and some distant gentle hills.
There's nothing sinister, nothing to worry about.

But in the dark Karen thinks
the darting shapes on the ceiling
are really the shadows of a ghost's
great cold hands and that the night noises
made by the water pipes are the
screeches and groans of attic skeletons.

Count me Out

One football player scored his second goal,
Two card sharpers did a three-card trick,
Three little babies crawled on all-fours,
Four office clerks worked a five-day week,
Five clucky chickens laid half-a-dozen eggs,
Six Mars Bars and I'm in seventh heaven,
Seven Scottish dancers did an eightsome reel,
Eight black cats with nine lives each,
Nine shopkeepers out to lunch, back at ten to...
...One football player scored his second goal...

The sun wakes up

The sun wakes up
Yes, the sun wakes up.

The sun it smiles
Yes, the sun it smiles.

The wind it blows
Yes, the wind it blows.

The clouds come over
Yes, the clouds come over.

The rain falls down
Yes, the rain falls down.

The earth dries up
Yes, the earth dries up.

The sun lies down
Yes, the sun lies down.

The dark moves in
Yes, the dark moves in.

The moon looks up
Yes, the moon looks up.

The night lies still
Yes, the night lies still.

The old folk die
Yes, the old folk die.

The sun wakes up
Yes, the sun wakes up.

WHOO
In the graveyard at night
When the full moon's bright,
You may see something scary movering.
Don't scream or yell
Or clang the church bell
Cause it's only the ghosties whoovering.

Schlurp, Schlubble

My mother knew a lot about manners,
She said you should never slurp;
You should hold your saucer firmly
And not clang your teeth on the curp.

My father knew nothing of manners,
All he could do was burp;
So when I can't find a rhyming word
I set about making them urp.

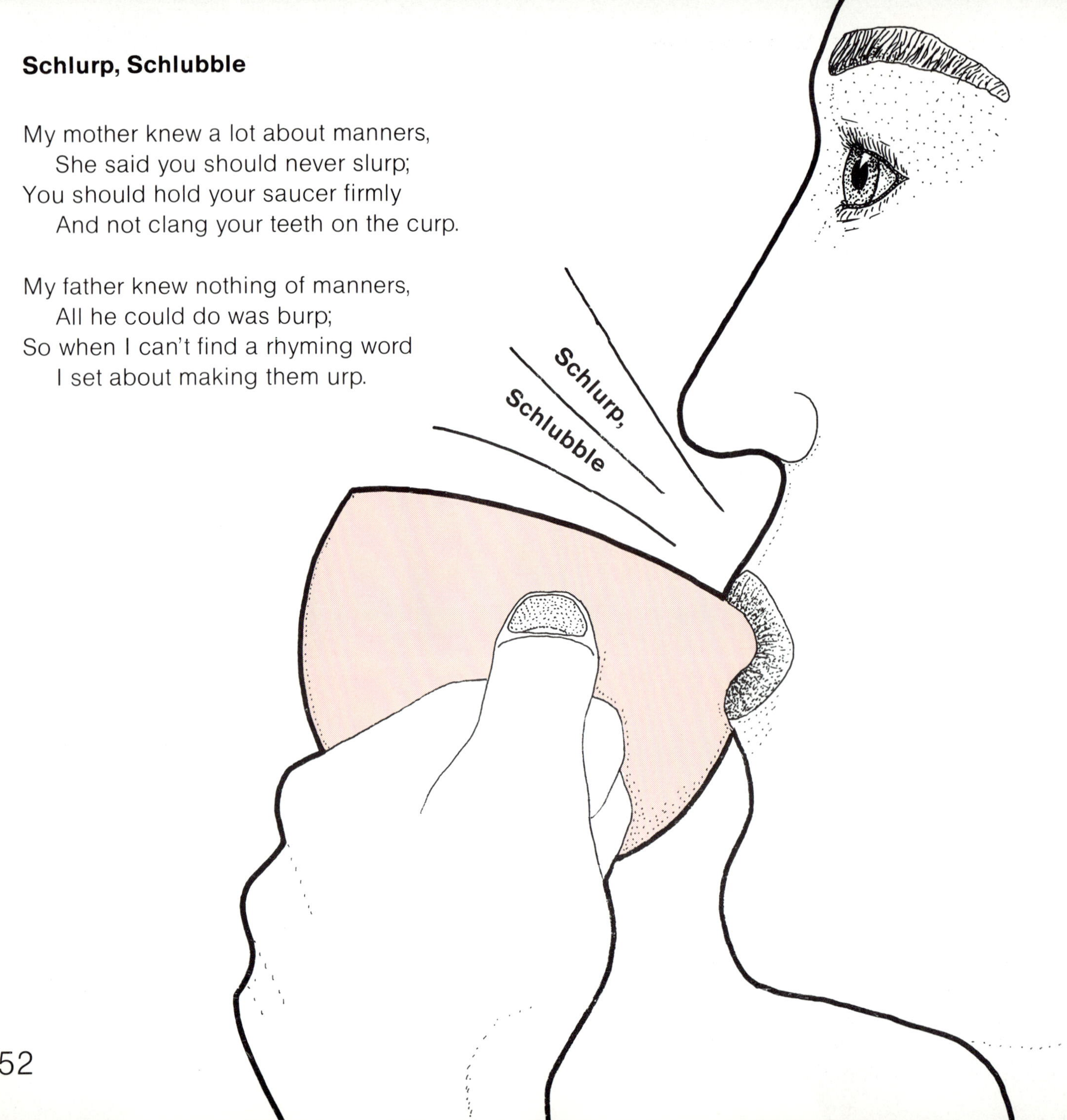

Do You Know What My Father Did?

Last night it was really hot
and we got back late from the beach
and my brother and sister and I
were really starving and my father said
that we couldn't be cause if we were
hungry we'd have eaten more sandwiches
on the picnic instead of eating all those
crisps and chocolate biscuits.
Anyway we asked for some supper in bed
and he said "No!" and he told me
to feed the bloomin' cat cause he was
fed up listening to the bloomin' thing
meowing all over the place and he was
really sick of it. He says the only
time he ever sees it is when it
stretches its dirty paws up the fridge
door looking for food.

Do you know what my father did?

Well when we were in bed moaning about
not getting any supper even though
Sian Fuggle says she gets sweets and
lemonade **every** night just before she
goes to bed – my father came up with
three plates with a piece of bread on
each one. He said "Here's some supper,
eat this up, it's good for you."
We said when we looked at it closely
and had looked at each other,
"Yeuch – it's catfood!"
He said, "Don't be silly, its patē."
I said "it's more like cow patē!"

"Eat it up." said my mother who was sitting on the stairs trying not to laugh. We all shouted things like "We're not eating catfood sandwiches!"

Do you know what my father said?

He said his Uncle John used to take a packed lunch to work every day (he also said his Uncle John worked for a banana company and could get huge bunches of bananas for nothing and he'd give them away to children on the street) and one day his Aunt Pearl forgot to get anything for Uncle John's sandwiches – no cheese, cold meat or chicken paste or anything like that. So she just got some catfood from the cupboard and spread it on some bread. When her husband came home from work that night he said, "Those sandwiches were delicious, have you got any more of that meat for tomorrow?" So Uncle John got catfood on his sandwiches quite often and he liked it so we should too. Well we didn't eat it and my sister took the sandwiches downstairs to Gogo cat but even he wouldn't eat the meat.

Later my mother brought us up a snack; bread and jam, a Jaffa biscuit, a slice of apple and a bit of melon.
Do you know what my father did?
He came up and read us some poems.

Rockets and Quasars

Planets and Stars,

I'm fed up with Earth

So I'll see you on Mars...